I live with JESUS

Éditions Paulines

This book originally appeared as *Je vis avec Jésus*, Anne Sigier, Québec, 1990.

Phototypesetting: *Éditions Paulines*

Texts: *Anne Sigier*

Cover and drawings: *Éric Sigier*

ISBN 2-89039-569-3

Legal deposit — 4th Quarter 1992
Bibliothèque nationale du Québec
National Library of Canada

© 1992 Éditions Paulines
        250, boul. Saint-François Nord
        Sherbrooke, QC, J1E 2B9

CONTENTS

1. INTRODUCTION

2. THE ENCOUNTER

3. THE KINGDOM

4. THE WORD

5. FORGIVENESS

6. THE LIBERATION

7. SUFFERING

8. THE FAMILY

9. LIFE WITH JESUS

"I live with Jesus"

The title of this book is no doubt an occasion of hope for you.

You know deep down that to live with Jesus is to know peace, it is to live in harmony with others, it is to welcome the one who is different from you, it is to forgive the one who has hurt you.

To live with Jesus is to listen to his Word, it is to speak to him in prayer, it is to gradually become his hands, his gaze, it is to accept others as He did. It is to have his spirit.

What is the meaning of your life today?
Who is Jesus for you?
Are you thoroughly happy or do you experience a fleeting, uneventful happiness; are you begging right and left for affection, in search of new tricks to be happy?
What do you seek? Whom are you looking for?

This book would simply like to shed some light on some of Jesus' words so that today they may be a light on your path, a consolation in your sadness, a presence in your solitude.

This book will speak to you about certain people whose lives were touched by a Word of God, or by a contact with Jesus during his public life.

This book will also speak of you. You will rediscover yourself in these pages. You will see how important you are in the eyes of God.

Examine the drawings carefully, note the presence of trees in most of the encounters: the Tree of Life is Jesus.

The drawings were made by Eric, a young father of three children, a "trucker" by trade. He drives big trucks. During his long journeys, he observes people and nature a great deal. He agreed to make the drawings, even if that is not his profession, because he knows that without Jesus, it is very difficult to live in truth today.

You will see that the texts are often written in the masculine form, but it is very obvious that this book is as much for girls as it is for boys.

It is addressed to all the adolescents who are in search of a true friend, of someone whose Word is both demanding and enlightening. Someone who knows both the profound needs of young people and also all the temptations of the world of today.

This book speaks of the love and mercy of Jesus. It reminds us that God always fulfils his promises; that Jesus rose from the dead; that the Holy Spirit is present in the Church.

You will see that, page by page, you will find a little something of your life. You will recognize your friends, you will understand that Jesus alone, by the truth of his Word and by the love he has for you, can say to you again today:

> Stand up, son of man,
> Come with me, come live with me.
> There lies your happiness.

1

Introduction

In the beginning
  God created the heavens, the earth,
    light, night and day.

He created the waters, the trees, the moon and the sun,
  the stars, the animals.

Then God created man in his own image,
  in the image of God he created him.

God saw everything that he had made:
  and he saw that everything was good.

Genesis 1

You, too, were already foreseen in the harmony of this creation.

God put the tree of life in the middle of the garden.
He set there the tree of the knowledge of good and evil.

God gave the man this commandment:
    "You may eat of every tree of the garden.
    But of the tree of the knowledge of good and evil you shall not eat.
    For the day that you eat of it, you shall die."

The serpent, the devil, deceived the man and the woman, Adam and
Eve:
    "If you eat of this tree, you will not die.
    You will be like gods who know good and evil."
Adam and Eve listened to the serpent:
they thought they would find a happiness greater
    than that of living in the presence of God.

They disobeyed and immediately they knew the shame
of their nakedness; they hid themselves and they were afraid.

Genesis 3

The devil is the one who seduced Adam and Eve; he wanted to bring
   them away from God.
He is still the one today who tries to take me away
   from the presence of Jesus in me.

I no longer take time to admire nature.
I no longer take time to listen to the essential things in life.

The others around me run about, are busy,
flee away from themselves in work, meetings, games, television, etc.

Noise, speed, excitement, money, stimulants...
All that clutters up my heart in spite of myself.

So then I set the volume of music very loud...
It is easier not to hear the others, nor even to listen
   to my own sadness and solitude.

"I have seen the misery of my people
and I have heard their cry", says the Lord.

Take time to look, to listen, to be in wonder.

You will see that it is possible to find happiness today.

The tree of life is always in the midst of the garden of the world.

The tree of life is God in your life.

2

The Encounter

In the Gospel, Jesus often speaks of happiness.
He says they are happy those who have the soul of the poor,
who are gentle,
who are merciful,
who are pure,
who are peacemakers.

He also says that even those who are sad,
those who suffer for the sake of justice
are happy because they are called the sons of God.

To understand Jesus, it is enough to listen to him like a little child
who allows himself to be led in total trust.

He speaks to simple hearts, he, the king of Israel, who enters Jerusalem
humbly riding a donkey.

Jesus walked along through towns and villages.
His apostles loudly proclaimed:
> "Repent and put your faith in the Gospel."

Jesus says that if you believe, you will be saved.

Because if you believe that God, your Father, freely loves you such as
you are, if you believe that he sends Jesus to take
all your miseries and your sins upon himself
and that he has triumphed over death by raising Jesus from the dead,
if you believe, you have eternal life.

People around Jesus, as around yourself, would like to believe,
but they hesitate, they are afraid,
they are waiting for someone to take the step along with them
to lead them to Jesus.

Jesus always comes to meet us.

One day when Paul was setting out to wage war against Jesus' friends, he was thrown down to the ground and a great light from heaven surrounded him in a dazzling brilliance.
— Saul, why are you persecuting me?
— Who are you, Lord?
— I am Jesus whom you are persecuting. But get up; enter the city and you will be told what you must do.

When I am deep in sadness and in darkness because of sin,
when I hurt others with my lies and my selfishness,
Jesus tells me: "I am the one to whom you are doing these evil things."
But he adds straightaway: "Get up. Listen to my word."

I know that if I listen to Jesus, if I obey his word,
I remain in his light.

Acts 9

26

For three days, Paul could not see anything. He was blind.
He stayed in Damascus and neither ate nor drank.

The Lord sent Ananias, a disciple, to search for Paul:
"Go and lay your hands on him so that he may recover his sight.
This man is an instrument I have chosen to proclaim my name
before pagan nations, kings and the sons of Israel."

Ananias obeyed the Lord, in spite of his fear of meeting Paul:
everyone knew about his hatred for Christians.
Ananias laid his hands on him and said:
"Paul, my brother, the Lord is sending me so that you may regain
your sight. Be filled with the Holy Spirit."

Paul immediately could see. He was baptized on the spot
and he set out to proclaim everywhere that Jesus is the Son of God.

Jesus also invites those who are the greatest sinners
to become the greatest saints.

Acts 9

Filled with the Holy Spirit, Paul set out to proclaim the love
and the forgiveness of Jesus throughout the world.

He also wrote to his Roman, Corinthian, Galatian, Colossian friends,
to keep their faith alive, to help them live according to the spirit of
Jesus.
His letters, called epistles, are the testimony of his journey in faith.

Saint Paul says:
"I would like to do what is right, but evil suggests itself to me. My
inner being delights in the law of God. But I notice another law at
work in my body, a law that fights against the law my mind approves
of. It makes me a prisoner to the law of sin which is at work in my
body."

Sometimes it happens that I, too, cannot do the good I would like to do,
I reject friendship, I want to be independent or selfish...
others judge me and I am miserable.

Romans 7

I find myself again all alone and I no longer understand myself.
I see how true it is that on my own I can do nothing.

Then, I cry to the Lord:
"Jesus, you can do everything. Come to my help, have mercy on me."

The Lord always listens to the prayer of the one
who asks him for his Spirit.

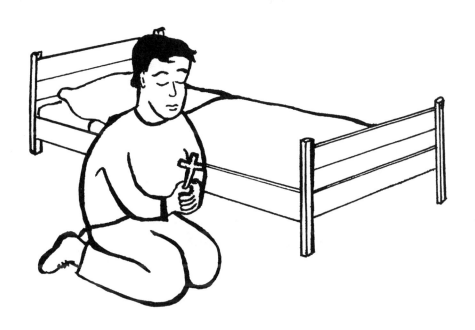

One day, Jesus was coming out of Jericho.

There was a large crowd around him.
By the roadside, a blind man, Bartimaeus, was begging.

When he heard the crowd passing by, he knew that Jesus was not far.

Then he began to shout:
"Lord Jesus, son of David, have mercy on me!"

Some wanted to quieten him down because his shouts were annoying
to them. But he shouted all the more loudly:
"Lord Jesus, have mercy on me!"

Then Jesus stood still.

Luke 18

Jesus said to his disciples: "Bring him to me."
The disciples went to the blind man:
"Have courage, have faith, the master is calling you."

"What do you want me to do for you?" asked Jesus.
— Master, let me see again!
— Go, your faith has saved you.

Immediately, Bartimaeus regained his sight and he followed Jesus.

Jesus always listens to the one who cries out to him.

He is inviting you to allow yourself to be healed by him if you are suffering.
Sometimes you can no longer see your way in life: the world tells you
use violence, you will be the strongest,
cheat, you will come out first,
indulge in every pleasure possible, life is so short...

Deep down, you know that Jesus is the light. He is asking you:
"What do you want me to do for you?"

When Jesus invites someone to live with him, he often calls
   the brothers, the sisters, the whole family as well.

When Jesus was walking by the sea of Galilee,
he saw two brothers: Simon, called Peter, and Andrew, his brother.
They were fishermen.
He said to them: "Come, follow me, and I will make you fishers of men."

Immediately, they left their nets to follow him.

As he went a little farther, he saw two other brothers, James and John.
"You, too, come with me."

They left their boat and followed him.

Jesus still passes by today and he still calls us.

Will I be lucky enough to hear his voice
   in all the hurly-burly of my life?

Mark 1:16

Jesus said to his disciples:
"If anyone wishes to be my disciple,
let him take his cross and follow me.
Whoever loses his life because of me and the Gospel will save it."

Peter, James and John were listening...

One day, Jesus went out to a lonely spot on a high mountain.
He brought along the three disciples to pray with him.

Suddenly, Jesus was transfigured before their very eyes:
his clothes became white as snow, dazzling white.

A cloud came and overshadowed them and a voice said:
"This is my beloved Son, listen to him!"

God, Jesus' Father, our Father, confirms the love he has for his Son.
He tells us: "Listen to him."

Luke 9:28

To become a true leader, a true servant,
Simon Peter learned from Jesus how to acknowledge
what comes from God.

Jesus explained to his disciples that in order that the Kingdom
might come, he had to give up his life and die for all men.

Simon Peter did not understand.
He did not want Jesus to die; he had failed to understand that
God could make life spring forth from death.

Jesus rebuked Peter:
"Get behind me, Satan! For your thoughts are not
on the things of God, but on the things of men!"

Sometimes, you find that the words of the Gospel are difficult to live by.
You would even like to be able to change them.
"I will send you my Spirit who will make you understand everything",
says Jesus.

Mark 8:31

Simon Peter betrayed Jesus at the time of his passion.
"No, I do not know this man," he said three times.
Then, he was very sorry for his sin.

One day, after his resurrection, Jesus joined Peter on the shore
of the Lake Tiberias and asked him also three times:
— Simon Peter, do you love me?
— You know everything, Lord, you know I love you.
— Feed my lambs.

This text from the Gospel of Saint John is the most beautiful proof of the
total forgiveness granted by Jesus to the one who is sorry for his sins.
Jesus gives you again his total trust every time you tell him:

"Lord, you know I love you."

John 21

When he wrote to his friends, Peter shared his life experience.
"With a pure heart, love one another.
In a spirit of unity in brotherly love, in mercy,
with a humble mind, do not repay evil for evil.
On the contrary, repay with a blessing, for that is what you have
been called to do
so that you might inherit the blessing."

Bless the Lord for the day you were born,
bless him for your parents, your brothers and sisters,
for your friends, for your enemies,
for your teachers,
for the joys and the pains.
Bless him for all the things you have.
Bless him also for all the things you do not have.

At all times, bless the Lord.

1 Peter 3

Jesus had twelve apostles:
    Simon Peter, James and John,
    Andrew, Philip and Bartholomew,
    Matthew, Thomas, James son of Alphaeus,
    Thaddaeus, Simon the Zealot,
    and Judas.

They are the ones to whom Jesus entrusted his Kingdom.

"Go to the lost sheep of the House of Israel.
What you are to say will be given you at that time,
    for it is not you who will speak, but the Spirit of your Father
      who will speak through you.
Take no bag nor purse,
    nor two tunics nor a staff,
For the laborer deserves his food.
Whoever loses his life because of me will find it again."

Matthew 10

3

The Kingdom

"Do not let your heart be troubled!
You believe in God, believe also in me," says Jesus.
"There are many dwellings in my Father's house. I am going to prepare
a place for you. You know the way to the place where I am going."

Thomas said to him: "Lord, we do not know where you are going.
How could we know the way?"

"I am the Way, the Truth, the Life.
No one comes to the Father except through me.
If you love me, you will keep my commandments.
I will pray the Father and he will give you the Spirit of Truth.
I will not leave you orphans."

John 14

Jesus is addressing these same words to you.
Sure of his love, you can sing this beautiful psalm along with David:
"The Lord is my shepherd, there is nothing I shall want.
He leads me beside still waters; he restores my soul.
Even though I walk through the darkest valley, I fear no evil,
for you are with me."

Psalm 23

Jesus is the Way, the Truth, the Life.
He is the one who shows us the way to the Kingdom.
Through his words and his actions, he shows us the path to follow.

At the time of his last meal with his apostles, shortly before his passion,
Jesus took a basin and washed the feet of all his disciples.

He said to them:
"Do you understand what I have done to you?
You call me Master and Lord,
    and you are right, for that is what I am.
If, therefore, I have washed your feet,
    you also ought to wash one another's feet.
As I have loved you,
    you, too, should love one another."

John 13

By washing his disciples' feet,
  Jesus was giving the answer to their question:
    "Who is the greatest?"

    "The one who wishes to be the greatest
      must make himself the least.
    I am among you as the one who serves!"

"All that you do to the least of mine,
you do it to me," said Jesus.

Luke 22; Matthew 25

To be the least, to be the servant
is to choose the last place.

It means taking time to listen,
   taking time to love and share.
Sometimes, it means to expose ourselves to criticism
   in order to be a disciple of Jesus.

"If you wish to be the first, you must become everyone's servant."

Mark 10:44

I often think that in order to be first
I must be the most powerful.
And I am unhappy because I do not yet possess
    all I would like to have.

        I would like to have my friend's games.
        I would like to be the best in class.
        I would prefer my neighbor's house.

I would need a computer,
                a motorcycle,
                    some new friends...

I dream about all I would like to have
    and my heart is very empty.

Jesus has a story for you:

There was once a farmer who was very rich;
his fields had earned him much money.

He began to dream about having barns that would be still larger
to store all his grain.

He thought: "I am going to work like a fool
                to have as many possessions as possible,
                to have all the comfort,
                to be richer yet.
                I will be a powerful man.
                Others will look at me with envy."

Luke 12

"You fool!" God said to him.
"This very night you will die.
All the things you have gathered, who will get them?"

Jesus teaches us that to have many things
   does not make one happy.
True happiness does not lie there.

Saint Paul writes:
   "Those who want to be rich
   fall into temptation, fall into the trap of a host of desires
   that make people very unhappy.
   For the love of money is the root of all evils."

Have you ever noticed around you how quarrels
   often begin because of money?

To live with Jesus is to find joy.

To live with Jesus is to be certain that he loves you as you are:
    beautiful or handsome, not so beautiful or not so handsome,
    ill, in good health, crippled,
    with your triumphs, with your weaknesses.
He loves you if you are poor.
He loves you if you are rich.

When you are rejected by those you love, he welcomes you.
When you do not understand certain events, he listens to you.
When you do not know where to go, he is waiting for you.

"You are precious in my sight,
and honored, and I love you", says Jesus.

Isaiah 43

Jesus takes care of you.
You are very important to him.

To make you understand that, he tells you:
   "Consider the lilies of the fields,
      they are clothed more beautifully than princes.
   Consider the birds in the sky,
      God feeds them.
   How much more precious than the birds you are in the sight of God."

Do not worry, life is more important
   than food and clothing.

Do not fear, seek the Kingdom,
   that is, strive to have the Spirit of Jesus
   and all these things besides will be given to you.

Take time to discover nature,
you will understand how important you are to the Creator.

                                                              Luke 12:22

4

The Word

To seek the Kingdom also means to begin to listen attentively
   to the Word of God.

One day, Jesus was invited to eat at the home of Martha and Mary.
They were the sisters of Lazarus, a friend of Jesus.

Martha was getting worried in the kitchen
   as she was preparing the meal.

As for Mary, she was sitting at the Lord's feet.
   She was listening to him.

Luke 10:30

Martha was complaining and growing impatient
  because Mary was not helping her.

She asked Jesus:
    "Could you tell my sister to come and help me.
    I am doing all the work. Mary lets me serve all alone!"

Jesus answered:
    "Martha, Martha, you are worked up about many things.
    And yet, so little is needed,
      one thing alone is important.
    Mary has chosen the better part;
      it will not be taken away from her."

Luke 10:41

Mary found her joy in listening to the Lord.
Everything else was of secondary importance.

Meeting God in his Word and in the sacraments to discover day by day
the true meaning of life, of work, of friendship, of sharing, is a thing of
great importance.

In the Church, there are people who devote their time
    to listening and praying to the Lord.
These contemplative people carry all the problems of the world in
their prayer. Often they will till the land, or do crafts to provide for
their needs. Their priority is to live in God.

Still today, many young people love to spend long hours
    in the silence of a monastery.
When they are in a state of uncertainty, or too tempted by the
    deceptive pleasures of life,
when they want to pray or reflect,
    they find there a profound peace, as answer to their need for God.

In order to help you understand well the importance of the Word of God,
   Jesus tells this story:

The sower went to sow his seed.
The seed is the Word of God.

The seed fell on the roadside and the birds ate it.
Or the seed fell on rocky soil, it started to grow and then withered.
There were no roots. The plant died.

They are the ones who hear my word,
   who receive it with joy for a while,
   but they cease to believe as soon as they are ridiculed because of me.
They are also the ones who allow themselves to be distracted
   by all sorts of idols.

Luke 8

There are other seeds that fall in the soil
  among brambles and thorns.

The plants grow but they are choked by the thorns.

They are the ones who hear the Word of God,
but they are too weak to say no
  when temptation comes.

It is the Evil One who takes away the Word from their heart,
for fear they might believe and be saved.

There are also the seeds that fall in good soil.

The one who listens to Jesus, who listens to his brothers,
the one who, at home, at work, or in his leisure time,
    day after day, tries to say yes to everything Jesus expects of him,
the one who does not hesitate to give his life to proclaim the Good News,
that one is the good soil
    that allows itself to be watered by the Word of the Gospel.

To be the good soil is to believe that Jesus
is able to heal you of all your weaknesses.
It is to believe that he died and rose from the dead so that you
    may have life.

5

Forgiveness

To discover this immense love Jesus has for us,
you sometimes need the help of others.

One day, a paralyzed man was brought by his friends
    to the house where Jesus was.
There were many people gathered there.

Since it was impossible to come near Jesus,
the friends of the paralyzed man climbed onto the roof
    and made an opening in it to bring down the sick man
    right in front of Jesus.

They were so sure that Jesus could heal him.

Mark 2

Jesus was touched by the faith of these men.
He said to the paralytic:
"My child, your sins are forgiven.
Stand up, take your mat and walk."

When you receive forgiveness from Jesus,
you are healed of your most profound infirmities,
those that bind your heart in chains.

"I will put my spirit in you
and make you live according to my laws.
I will cleanse you from all your sins.
You will be my people and I shall be your God."

Ezechiel 36

Sometimes, you, too, feel like a cripple.

When you have lied, it is as if your eyes were sore;
  you no longer dare look straight at the other.

When you have spoken ill of someone,
  you find it difficult to walk near that person.

When you have stolen, when you have hurt, when you have cheated,
  your heart is no longer free, you are bound, as it were.

In the sacrament of forgiveness, Jesus, through his disciple,
  loosens your bonds, restores your freedom.

  My child, stand up, take whatever makes you suffer,
  you are no longer alone, go forth with me.

Jesus is the resurrection,
that is, he always makes us go from death to life.

Jesus had a friend. His name was Lazarus.
He was the brother of Martha and Mary.

It happened that Lazarus died.

It was the custom among the Jews
to wrap the dead person with strips of cloth;
then he was put in a cave
and a large stone was rolled in front of it.

John 11:1

Jesus arrived in front of the tomb of his friend.
"Take away the stone," he said.

Then he prayed God his Father and praised him for all he had done.

He shouted: "Lazarus, come out!"

Lazarus came out. His friends freed him from all his strips of cloth.

As in the case of the paralytic, Lazarus was helped by the others.
The others are the Church:
   those who believe in the power of the Holy Spirit.

John 11:43

It is always a great feast in the Kingdom of God
whenever a sinner is forgiven and turns to Jesus.

You know the story of the lost sheep?

A man had a hundred sheep.

One day, one of them got lost.
The man looked everywhere for it,
    leaving the other ninety-nine alone in the fold for a while.

When he found the lost sheep again, he carried it on his shoulders,
    all in joy,
and brought it back home.

Luke 15:4

To make us really understand the immense love his Father
    has for each one of us,
Jesus tells this other story:

A man had two sons.
The younger of the two decided to leave his home
    and asked for the share of the money that was coming to him.
The older son stayed home and worked with his father.

The younger son left;
he thought he was free: no more brother to disturb him,
                        no more authority to give
                            advice or tell him what to do.

He spent his money in gambling;
He went to disreputable places,
he idled away his time, let himself go,
he did all the things he wanted to do...

Luke 15:11

... but he was profoundly unhappy.

He had no money left. He was hungry.
He remembered his father.

"How mistaken I have been.
I thought that, on my own, I could have organized my life,
    have a taste of freedom.
I squandered everything.
I will go back to my father
    and I will ask him to forgive me."

His father saw him coming from afar. He ran to his son, put his arms around him and gave him a long hug.

— Father, I have sinned against heaven and against you. I am no longer worthy to be called your son.

The father pulled him up on his feet and cried out:
"This son of mine who was dead is alive again.
He was lost and is found again!
Come and eat at my table.
Your place is always there with me.
We are going to celebrate your return."

Jesus sees you from afar when you are walking towards him.

He is the one who runs out to meet you and to say:

"My child, you were lost, now you are found again,
you were suffering and you have found a new taste for life.
You always have a place with me."

6

The Liberation

From the very beginning, God has answered the prayer of those
   who beg to be freed from their enslavement.
In the Book of Exodus, it is written
   that the Israelites were prisoners in Egypt.

Every day, they had to work hard making bricks.
They were maltreated, they were beaten.
They could no longer put up with this.

They cried out and their call rose up to God from the depths
   of their misery.

God said to Moses:
   "I have seen the misery of my people.
   I have heard their cry; indeed, I know their sufferings.
   I want to deliver my people.
   Go, I am sending you to Pharaoh,
   bring my people out of Egypt."

Exodus 1 – 3

Moses came to Pharaoh and said to him:
"Thus speaks the God of Israel:
let my people go,
so that they may celebrate a festival for me in the desert."

Pharaoh refused to listen.
He became twice as mean towards the Israelites
and did not let them go.

God said to Moses:
"Prepare to leave Egypt in haste.
I shall strike the houses of the Egyptians,
but your houses, which will be marked with the blood of the lamb,
I will spare."

Exodus 12

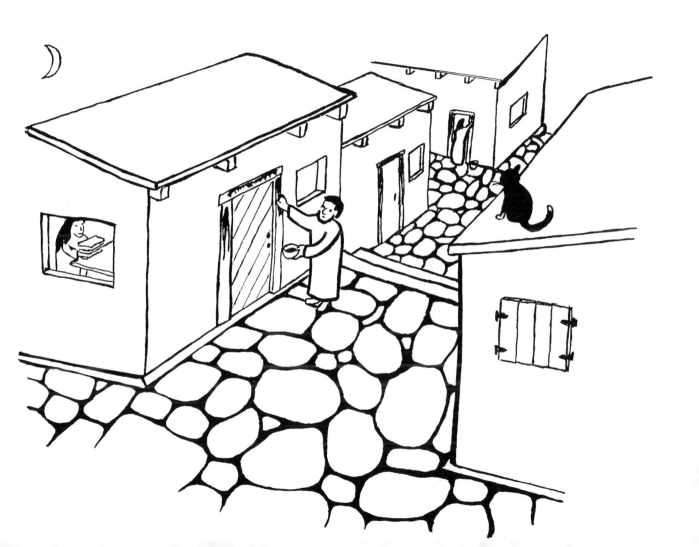

Pharaoh yielded before the God of Israel who was stronger than he.

"Rise and go away from my people,
and go and worship God as you have requested.
Begone and bring a blessing on me, too," said Pharaoh to Moses.

All the people came out in haste from the land of slavery,
bringing the bread which had had no time to rise,
   the unleavened bread.

But later, Pharaoh changed his mind;
with his entire army, he pursued Israel
   who was camping by the Red Sea.

When they saw the Egyptians launched in their pursuit,
the children of Israel were in great fear and Moses cried out to God:
      "Lord, come and save us!"

Exodus 14

Moses said to the people:
   "Do not fear; stand firm and you will see
   what God will do to save you today.
   God will fight for you; you have only to keep still."

Then God said to Moses:
   "Stretch out your hand and divide the sea
   so that my people may pass."

Moses stretched out his hand,
   and God drove back the sea with a strong wind blowing all night.
All the people crossed the sea on dry ground.

Then the waters came back upon Pharaoh and all his army.
All were swallowed up by the waves of the sea.

Exodus 14

On that day, God opened up a passage through the waters of death.
He saved the people of Israel from the slavery of the Egyptians.

The enemy was destroyed.
He threw horse and rider into the sea.

Moses and the Israelites sang in honor of God:
"Your love has led this people whom you redeemed,
your strength has guided it to your holy abode.
You will reign forever and ever."

In the waters of baptism, Jesus opens up a passage to every Christian
who wishes to live this covenant
and be delivered by him from all the slavery of sin.

In our everyday life,
God is the one who opens up a passage
so that you will not let yourself be stopped by obstacles.

Sometimes you feel timid,
   not so intelligent,
   weaker than the others.

God helps you reach out your hand
so that you may enjoy the taste of hospitality and friendship.

Sometimes the lack of knowledge about God, the fear of life,
or the hurts of childhood
    harden the heart.

Very quickly, you are carried along in the paths of darkness
and you come across violence, revenge, deceit, death.
You are caught up in a tide of competition, of debts, of fear,
    and the search for sensations
which might fulfil this immense need to be loved.

All your past matters little: you are a son of God.
And God loves you today.

Mary, the mother of Jesus and the mother of all human beings
    is watching over you;
as soon as you turn to her,
she guides you to the source of all forgiveness and of all joy:
    her son Jesus.

From the enslavement of drugs, the Lord delivers you.
From the enslavement of alcohol, the Lord delivers you.
From the enslavement of money, the Lord delivers you.

He is the one who leads from slavery to freedom,
from distress to joy,
from darkness to light.

Jesus Christ is the one who passed from death to life.
He is the Passover, the passage.

Risen from the dead, he is always by your side.

When you pray God your Father saying:
    "Your kingdom come",
You are asking him that, little by little,
his Spirit may penetrate all hearts
so that meanness, selfishness and deceit
may yield to meekness, to sharing and to truth.

There where the Spirit of the Lord is, there lies true freedom.

Jesus again says in the Gospel:
    "Love your enemies.
    Do good to those who hate you."

You know that unless the strength of the Spirit be in you,
You are unable to make these words come true.
Jesus alone, in you, can love
the one who has betrayed, who has hurt, who has deceived.

Jesus is able to heal the hurts in your painful memories.
Ask him for his Spirit of forgiveness
so that, someday, you may experience that it is possible, with him,
to forgive and love those who have harmed you.

Luke 6:27

7

Suffering

Illness, suffering, death
    make us cry out:
        "But why, Lord?
        Since you are infinitely good."

The silence of Jesus' answer
is experienced in the immense love with which he gives his life
on the cross for each one of us.

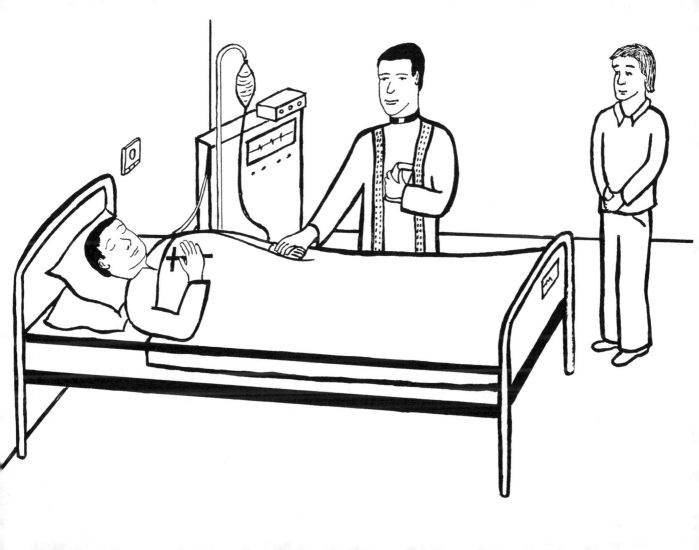

To live with Jesus is to believe in the risen Jesus.
It is to abandon ourselves to God day after day

knowing that when you weep, you are not alone,
             when you suffer, Jesus understands you:
He also wept when his friend Lazarus died.

Jesus walks at your side
   in your joys as in your griefs.

Do not heed the feelings of revolt that assail you
    when you can no longer put up with suffering.

Do not listen to the voice condemning you
    when you have done something wrong.

Accept in you Jesus who saves you.

He knows your suffering well,
he who descended into the hell of each man,
    into what is most painful to bear,
to take with him the evil in man
    and transform it into a resurrection.

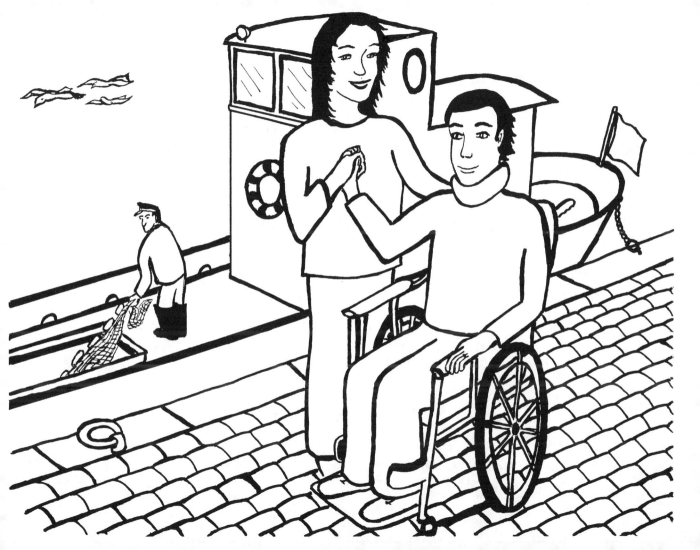

Sometimes, at the time of an accident,
of a stroke or paralysis, of an illness,
you feel you are at a loss, you do not understand.
Is God the one who wanted that?
Why?

The sick, the lame who live as disciples of Jesus have a mission.
They manifest the love of God:
"I will tell of your name to my brothers and sisters,
in the midst of the congregation, and I will praise you.
Praise the Lord.
He did not despise the affliction of the poor,
nor hide his face from him,
but, called upon by him, he heard his cry.
All the ends of the earth shall remember
and turn back to the Lord.
May your heart live forever!"

Psalm 22

Suffering is very real all around us.
Sometimes, people dare not speak about it,
   they fear they will not be understood.

Some types of suffering
   like solitude, rejection, indifference, remorse,
are sometimes more painful than illness.

Do not lose heart, keep your eyes fixed on Jesus.

"If I could only touch his cloak,"
said this woman who had been suffering for a long time,
"I would be made well."

"Be healed, your faith has saved you," Jesus said to her.

Matthew 9:21

When you are punished unjustly,
   Jesus sees you as his brother.
Do not hold a grudge.

Be happy when you create
   harmony and peace around you
because you will be called a son of God.

Sometimes you think
   that nobody loves you,
   that nobody understands you.

You turn in upon yourself,
you no longer want to share,
you lose your smile,
you feel useless.

Helping others is the opportunity for you
to find your own joy again.

"You shall love your neighbor as yourself."

That is "living the Law in its plenitude," says Saint Paul.

Galatians 5:14

Jesus is the one who reconciles all things to himself.

He breaks down the barriers
   that sometimes separate us from each other.

With him, it is possible to ask one another to be forgiven.

   "Come to terms with God, and be at peace;
   in this way your happiness will again be yours."

Colossians 1:20; John 22:21

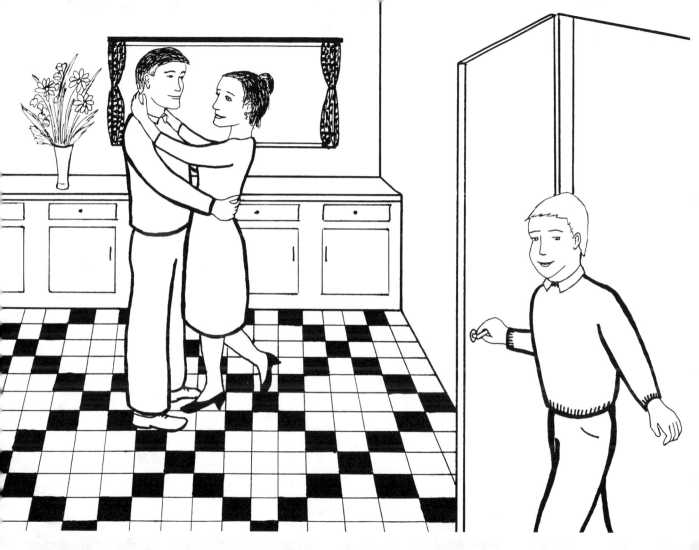

8

The family

"Fulfil my joy completely by being united amongst yourselves.
Let the love of everyone of you for one another be the same.
Live in peace. Rejoice always.
Give thanks in all circumstances."

1 Thessalonians 5

In the simple day to day life,
with your parents, with your grandparents,
you have a taste of the peace of God
    when you seek to make others happy.

Sometimes, people think that children
    are annoying to elderly persons.
So we place them in homes for the elderly.
Grandparents say they prefer the noise and the hugs of children
    to the loneliness and the silence of their room in such homes.

Happy the man who finds his joy in his children!
Children are a gift from God.

Psalm 127

Children, obey your parents in the Lord: for this is right.
Honor your father and your mother,
  so that it may be well with you
  and that you may live long on earth.

And you, parents, do not provoke your children to anger,
but bring them up
in the discipline and instructions of the Lord.

Ephesians 6

All the families of the earth shall be blessed!

Acts 3:25

"Kindness to parents will not be forgotten,
   but will serve as reparation for your sins.
On the day of your trial, God will remember you.
Whoever deserts a father is no better than a blasphemer,
   and whoever distresses his mother is cursed by the Lord.
For the Lord honors the father in his children
   and confirms a mother's rights over her children."

Ecclesiasticus 3

You see how the family is important in the eyes of God.
Today, however, too many families are broken.
Separation and divorce cause distress in the children.

Jesus accompanies and comforts those who weep,
   "Come to me, all you who are weary and are carrying heavy burdens,
   and I will give you rest."

Matthew 11:28

He also says: Do not judge so that you may not be judged."

Matthew 7:1

154

"I will not leave you orphaned. I will come to you."

John 14:18

It is through the love and the hospitality found in the hearts of families
that Jesus comes to comfort the orphaned child.

"All you will do to the least of mine,
you will be doing unto me."

If you offer your food to the hungry,
and satisfy the needs of the afflicted,
then your light shall rise in the darkness.
The Lord will guide you continually,
he will satisfy your needs in parched places,
and make your bones strong.
You shall be like a watered garden,
like a spring of water.
Your ancient ruins shall be rebuilt,
you shall be called the Repairer of the breach,
the Restorer of streets to live in.
You shall call the Lord, and he will answer: "Here I am."

Through the prophet Isaiah, God is the one suggesting
that you live in complete harmony with his will.

Isaiah 58

Remember your Creator in the days of your youth.

Jesus invites us to find happiness in his creation.
He makes available to you
   water, fire, nature, the air and the sun.
He also gives you brothers, sisters, friends,
   with whom you can share your joy.

   "Let no one despise your youth.
   On the contrary, set the believers an example
   in speech and conduct, in love, in faith, in purity.
   Pay close attention to yourself and to your teaching.
   Persevere in these dispositions.
   This is how you will find life."

1 Timothy 4

9

Life with Jesus

Paul writes to his friends and tells them:
    "Respect those who labor among you,
    and have charge of you in the Lord
    and admonish you.

    Esteem them very highly with great love because of their work.
    Be at peace among yourselves.
    Encourage the fainthearted,
    help the weak, be patient with all of them.

    May the Lord of peace himself sanctify you entirely
    and may your whole being,
    your spirit, your soul and your body,
    be kept blameless for the coming of our Lord Jesus Christ."

1 Thessalonians 5

"For the precept is a lamp,
the teaching is a light,
the reproofs of discipline are the way of life."

Proverbs 6:23

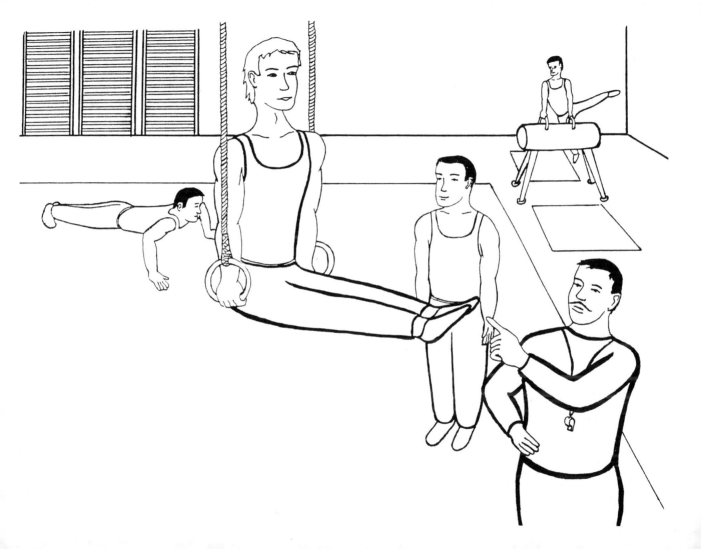

The ten commandments are also the way of life. God gave them to Moses saying to him: "I am your God who brought you out of the house of slavery." He helped us in our weakness by giving them to us.

You shall have only one God.	*There lies your happiness.*
You shall not blaspheme.	*There lies your happiness.*
You shall make holy the day of the Lord.	*There lies your happiness.*
You shall honor your father and your mother.	*There lies your happiness.*
You shall not kill.	*There lies your happiness.*
You shall not commit acts of impurity.	*There lies your happiness.*
You shall not steal.	*There lies your happiness.*
You shall not lie.	*There lies your happiness.*
You shall keep yourself from all impure	
thoughts, you shall not commit adultery.	*There lies your happiness.*
You shall not desire your neighbor's goods.	*There lies your happiness.*

God gives us the ten commandments so that we may live the Beatitudes and he tells us: "If you obey and put this law into practice, you will have a long life, you, your children and the children of your children. May you listen, keep and observe what will make you happy."

Deuteronomy 6

"God is our refuge and our strength,
a help always present in our trouble."

Psalm 46

Life comes from God.
God is Life.

Jesus accompanies expectant mothers with a great love.
They bear in themselves the child of God.

Even if the world suggests thousands of ways of killing life,
Jesus says again today as in the past, for the sake of your happiness:
"You shall not kill."

Therefore, choose life
so that you and your children may live
loving the Lord your God,
listening to his voice, holding fast to him:
for that is your life.

Deuteronomy 30:19-20

"My love for you is eternal",
says Jesus.

To those who believe in his name,
to those who accept him as Father,
God gives the power to become children of God.

"Here is my beloved, I have placed my Spirit on him.
I, the Lord,
I have called you by your name,
    you are mine.
You are very special in my sight,
you are important to me
    and I love you.
Your name is engraved on the palm of my hands,
    and I am with you."

I baptize you in the name of the Father and of the Son
    and of the Holy Spirit.

When, at the end of time,
the Lord calls those blessed by his Father,
he will say to all those who gave
of their time and of their love to the poor:
"Come, you who gave me to eat when I was hungry,
enter into the Kingdom of heaven!"

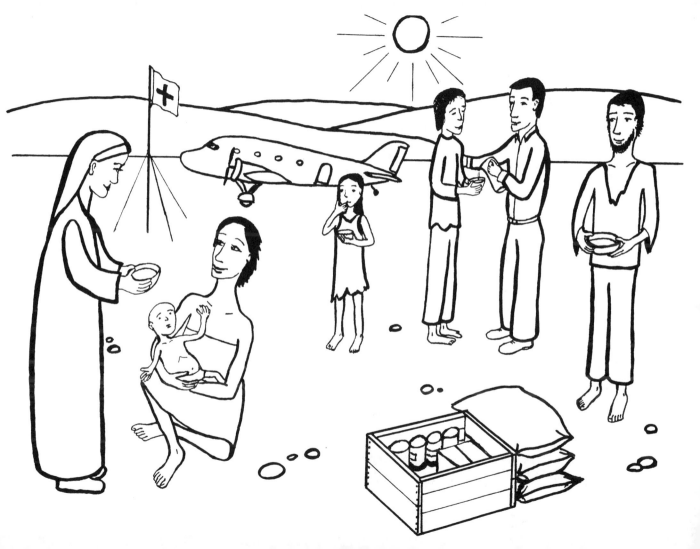

"The harvest is plentiful,
but the laborers are few.
Therefore, ask the Lord of the harvest
to send out laborers to his harvest.
I am sending you like lambs among wolves.
Carry no purse, no bag.
Whatever house you enter,
first say:
    Peace to this house!"

Luke 10

In order that the priest may continue his mission,
in order that he may remain attentive to everyone
and bring the Good News of the Love of God,
take time to pray the Lord:
    "Jesus, may your peace and your strength
    remain in the heart of all the priests."

"When you give alms,
let not your right hand know what your left hand is doing;
your Father who sees in your heart will return it to you."
"Never turn your face away from anyone who is poor,
and the face of God will not be turned away from you.
If you have much, give more, if you have little, give less,
but do not hesitate to give alms.
For almsgiving delivers from death,
it keeps you from going into the Darkness."

Tobit 4

You remember the story of the poor widow who gave all she had
to live on and that was only two small copper coins.
Jesus said: "Truly, I tell you, this widow, who is poor, has given
more than all the others; for they gave out of their abundance.
But she, in her poverty, gave all she had to live on."

Luke 21

Do you know that all you give in secret
will be given back to you a hundredfold by your Father who is in heaven?

One day, when it was very hot, Jesus, weary from his travels,
   arrived in Samaria.

A woman came to draw water from Jacob's well.
Jesus said to her: "Give me to drink."

By speaking to this Samaritan woman and asking her for water,
Jesus gives her the opportunity of entering into a dialogue with him;
   this will turn her life around.
The woman left her water jar right then and there and ran back
to the city to tell everyone:
      "Come and see a man who told me everything I had ever done.
      Could he not be the Christ?"

John 4

Jesus offers water that quenches all thirst to all those
      who have suffered, who have erred,
      who are exhausted, who are pointed at,
      who thirst for love.
This water springs into eternal life: this water is Jesus himself
who offers himself to you in the sacraments.

On two different occasions, on the day of his Baptism and on the day of his Transfiguration,
Jesus heard God, his Father, testifying to his love for him:
"You are my beloved Son. In you I have placed all my Love."

This is the love that was the source of life in Jesus.
Because he was sure of his Father's love for him,
Jesus was able to go through his passion
and die for us on the cross.

You, too, are a child of God,
and it is to you also that the Father says these words:
"You are my beloved child, in you I place all my love."

If you truly believe in this love, you will no longer fear.

You have seen that Jesus liberates from all enslavements.

He also frees the one who was possessed by an unclean spirit.

A man came to meet Jesus one day. He was shouting
    at the top of his voice.
He was mad, possessed by the devil.

"Come out of this man, you unclean spirit", said Jesus in a loud voice.

Mark 5

Coming out of him, the unclean spirit entered the swine
  who were feeding close by,
and the herd rushed down the steep bank into the sea.

The demoniac recovered his senses; he wanted to stay with Jesus.
But Jesus sent him on his mission:
    "Go home to your friends,
    and tell them all that the Lord has done for you
    in his mercy."

No sin, no power of evil can resist the love of God.
You can always cry out to Jesus: "Deliver me from evil!"

Nothing is impossible with God.

Jesus died but he rose from dead.
By his death and resurrection, Jesus assures you of life.
The resurrection of Jesus is, so to speak, a signature,
   giving authenticity to all the words of Christ:
it makes you enter into the tide of eternal life.

The Eucharist is the memorial of the death and resurrection of Jesus.
It is the sacrament of the body and blood of Jesus empowered
by the Spirit and offered to all men.
Jesus gives himself as nourishment,
   he gives himself abundantly so that you may live of his Spirit.

   "If you remember that your brother holds a grudge against you,
      leave your offering there and go and be reconciled to your brother."

Before I receive the Eucharist,
I enter into communion with those around me
or I become reconciled to those I have hurt,
so that I may live the words of Jesus in truth:
      "Love one another as I have loved you."

"Whoever eats of this bread will live forever.
And the bread I shall give
   is my flesh for the salvation of the world.
Whoever eats my flesh and drinks my blood
   has eternal life
and I shall raise him up on the last day."

"As you, Father, are in me and I in you,
may these also be in us,
so that the world may believe that you have sent me.

I have made your name known
   and I will make them know it,
so that the love you have given me
   may be in them
and I in them."

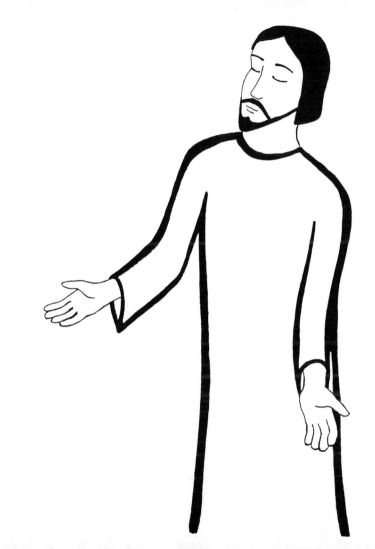

God, our Father, you gather us around your Son Jesus.
Teach us how to share,
give us the strength to forgive,
make us live the Love of the Risen One,
keep us in unity.
And we shall bear
   peace and hope to all the world!

May the Peace of Christ reign in your hearts!

Jesus has come to meet you in his Word.
You have read and listened to the things he had to tell you today.

Jesus loves you as you are;
   he is always there to greet you,
     to offer you his forgiveness,
     to tell you again that he loves you.
He walks before you, he knows the things that hurt you,
   he carries this cross with you,
   he teaches you to believe that his Father takes care of you,
     that you are his child.

Do not fear. Put your trust in him.
What he says is the truth.
What he offers you is life.

ALSO AVAILABLE:

I Meet Jesus
I Walk With Jesus

Achevé d'imprimer
en octobre 1992
sur les presses de
Imprimerie Métrolitho Inc.

Imprimé au Canada — Printed in Canada